I Can Find It!

Bible Stories

Publications International, Ltd.

Based on Bible stories. Illustrated by Stacy Peterson.
Additional images from Shutterstock.com.

Louis Weber, CEO
Publications International, Ltd.
8140 Lehigh Avenue
Morton Grove, IL 60053

This book conforms to the U.S. safety requirements of ASTM F963-16.

ISBN: 978-1-63938-836-3

Manufactured in China.

8 7 6 5 4 3 2 1

Let's get social!

 @Publications_International

 @PublicationsInternational

www.pilbooks.com

Table of Contents

The Creation Story

God created the whole world. He made the sky and land, the plants and animals, and the people too. But before God made the world, there was nothing. God was alone in the darkness. Then God said, "Let there be light." And there was light.

God called the light "day." When the light faded into darkness, God called it "night." It was the very first day of the world.

On the second day God created the water and sky. God called the water "the sea." He called the wide blue space above the water "the sky."

On the third day God created land. "Let there be dry land where the sea and sky meet," God said. And dry land appeared at once.

God shaped the land into tall mountains, deep valleys, and flat plains. He covered the land with beautiful green plants. Trees filled with fruit. Flowers bloomed in every color.

On the fourth day God hung the sun in the sky. He brightened the night sky with the moon and stars.

On the fifth day God filled the water with fish and created birds to soar through the sky. He made salmon and squid. He made white doves and colorful parrots.

On the sixth day God created animals to live on the land. God made alligators and ants. He made lions and lizards.

God was happy with all of the animals he had created. "That is good," God said. But something was still missing.

Then God made a man named Adam and a woman named Eve. God gave them a beautiful place to live called the Garden of Eden.

"You may eat anything in the garden," said God, "except for the fruit from this special tree." Adam and Eve promised not to eat from the special tree.

One day a snake tried to tempt Eve to eat from the special tree.

"If you eat fruit from this tree, you will become wise and powerful like God," said the snake.

Eve was tempted by the fruit on the special tree, which looked very tasty. So Eve took a bite. She gave some of the special fruit to Adam too.

God was very angry that Adam and Eve disobeyed him. He made Adam and Eve leave the Garden of Eden.

God created water, sky, and land. He covered the land in trees and flowers! Can you find everything you see in this box somewhere in the valley?

God created animals to live on the land and in the sky. He made gorillas and giraffes. God made cows and caterpillars. Can you find all the animals you see in this box somewhere in the picture?

Adam and Eve found special fruit on a special tree. They promised not to eat the special fruit. But Adam and Eve took a bite! Can you find everything you see in this box somewhere in the Garden of Eden?

Noah and the Ark

Once there was a man named Noah. Noah loved God. Noah also loved his family and neighbors. This made God happy. But God was unhappy with the people in the rest of the world.

God said to Noah, "I am going to wash away everything bad with a great flood."

God told Noah to build a big boat called an ark to save his family. "Bring two of every kind of animal onto the ark," God said. "And bring plenty of food for everyone."

Noah and his family started building the ark right away.

Noah's neighbors laughed when they saw what his family was building.

"Why do you need a big boat?" one neighbor chuckled. "You live in the desert!"

Noah warned other people about the flood, but no one listened. Noah and his family worked on the ark day and night. Finally, the ark was finished.

Then Noah's family gathered food to bring on the ark. They picked fruits, vegetables, and nuts. They stored enough food on the ark to feed Noah's family and the animals for a long time.

Noah gathered two of every kind of animal as God told him. The animals lined up in pairs. They boarded the ark two by two.

Once Noah and his family were safely on board the ark with the animals, it started to rain.

It rained without stopping for forty days and forty nights.

Soon water covered the entire Earth. Even the tallest mountains were underwater. Inside the ark the people and animals were safe.

After the rain stopped, the water slowly started to go down. The ark came to rest on top of a mountain.

Noah sent out a dove to search for dry land. The dove returned with a new olive leaf. This showed Noah that the land was dry and plants were growing again.

Noah knew it was finally safe to leave the ark. He and his family unloaded the animals onto dry land.

All the animals found new homes. The land was full of beautiful plants.

God promised Noah he would never again flood the entire Earth. "Whenever you see a rainbow in the sky," God said, "remember my promise."

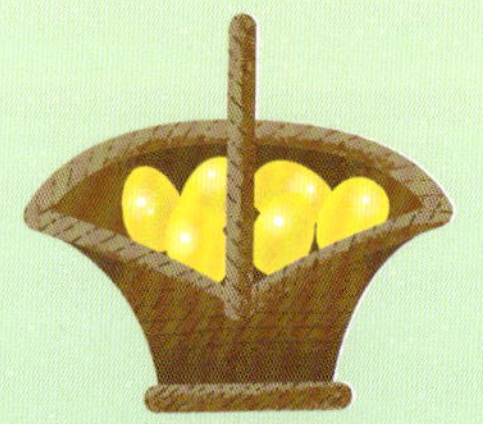

Noah's family found food to bring on the ark. They found enough to feed their family and the animals for many days and nights. Can you find everything you see in this box somewhere in the picture?

Noah found two of every kind of animal. The animals boarded the ark two by two. Can you find everything you see in this box somewhere around the ark?

The flood was over! Noah found dry land, and all the animals found new homes. Can you find everything you see in this box somewhere in the picture?

Joseph and His Colorful Coat

There once was a boy named Joseph. He had many brothers. Joseph and his brothers watched over their father's sheep. Their father, Jacob, loved Joseph best.

One day Jacob gave Joseph a present. It was a beautiful coat made of many colors.

"My favorite son deserves a special coat," Jacob said.

"I love it," said Joseph.

Joseph wore his special coat everywhere. This made Joseph's brothers angry because they wanted special coats too.

Whenever Joseph saw his brothers do something wrong, he would tell their father. His brothers were mad at Joseph for getting them in trouble. Everything Joseph did made his brothers upset.

One day while they watched the sheep, Joseph told his brothers about a dream he had.

"Each of us had a bunch of grain," Joseph said. "Then my bunch stood up. All of your bunches of grain bowed down to me."

This made his brothers even more angry than Joseph's special coat. "Do you think you are better than us?" one brother asked.

"Last night I had another dream," Joseph told his brothers a few days later. "The sun, moon, and stars bowed down to me," Joseph said. "Someday you will all bow down to me."

Joseph's brothers were furious. "We will never bow down to you," said one brother.

Later Jacob sent Joseph to check on his brothers, who were far away tending sheep. Joseph's brothers saw him in his colorful coat from a distance.

"Here comes the dreamer boy," one brother said. "We should get rid of him."

When Joseph arrived, his brothers ripped off his special coat. They threw him in an empty well.

"We shall see what comes of your dreams now," his brothers shouted into the well.

The brothers sat down to eat their dinner. As they were eating, they saw some travelers coming along.

"Let us sell our little brother to these traveling merchants," suggested one brother.

So the brothers sold Joseph to the merchants who were traveling to Egypt. The brothers returned home with Joseph's colorful coat.

"Where is Joseph?" their father asked. "We do not know," said one brother.

"We found his coat ripped up," said another brother. "He must have been eaten by a wild animal."

Jacob was very sad. He missed Joseph. After many years in Egypt, Joseph met his family again. He forgave his brothers and was again part of his family.

Joseph dreamed the sun, moon, and stars bowed down to him. Joseph told his brothers they would bow down to him too. This made his brothers furious! Can you find everything you see in this box somewhere in the picture?

Joseph found his brothers tending the sheep. They were still mad at Joseph. The brothers ripped off Joseph's colorful coat and threw him in a well! Can you find everything you see in this box somewhere in the picture?

The brothers met some traveling merchants from Egypt. They sold Joseph to the merchants. When Joseph saw his brothers many years later, he forgave them. Can you find everything you see in this box somewhere in the desert?

Moses and Miriam

Long ago, the Egyptians and Israelites lived happily together in Egypt. Then a bad Pharaoh came to power. He made the Israelites slaves.

The Pharaoh was unhappy. He thought there were too many Israelite slaves. So the Pharaoh gave a terrible order.

"Take every Israelite boy that is born away from his mother," the Pharaoh told his guards. "From now on, the Israelites may only have daughters."

Around this time there was an Israelite woman called Jochebed. She had a daughter named Miriam. Jochebed gave birth to a baby boy, Moses. To keep Moses safe, Jochebed and Miriam made a plan.

Jochebed sent Miriam to the river to collect reeds. Together, Jochebed and Miriam wove a sturdy basket from the reeds. They covered it with tar to make it waterproof. Jochebed put Moses in the basket and gave it to Miriam.

"Go to the river and hide the basket among the reeds," Jochebed told Miriam.

"Stay nearby," she told Miriam, "and watch over your brother."

"I will," Miriam promised.

Miriam watched as the basket floated toward some women who were swimming in the river. One of them was a princess, the Pharaoh's daughter.

The princess saw the basket and looked inside. Just then Moses started to cry. The princess was kind and felt sorry for him.

"He is one of the Israelite babies," the princess said.

Miriam rushed over to the princess. "Should I find a nurse to look after the baby for you?" Miriam asked.

"Yes," the princess answered.

Miriam ran to fetch her mother and brought her to the princess. "Will you take care of this baby for me?" the princess asked Jochebed.

"Yes!" Jochebed happily agreed. She would be able to care for her own son. Jochebed and Miriam thanked God that Moses was safe. They took Moses home.

When Moses was old enough, Jochebed brought him to the princess at the Pharaoh's palace. The princess adopted Moses and raised him as her own son.

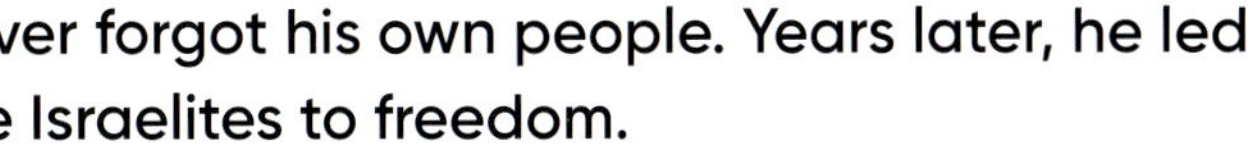

Moses grew up as a prince of Egypt, but he never forgot his own people. Years later, he led the Israelites to freedom.

The Pharoah gave a terrible order. He told his guards to find every Israelite boy and take the boys from their mothers. Can you find everything you see in this box somewhere around the palace?

The princess found baby Moses in a basket in the river. She told Miriam to find a nurse to care for the baby. She was a kind princess! Can you find everything you see in this box somewhere in the picture?

The princess adopted Moses when he was old enough. Jochebed and Miriam found comfort knowing Moses was safe. Can you find everything you see in this box somewhere in the picture?

David and Goliath

Once there was a shepherd boy named David. He watched over his father's sheep. David was the youngest and smallest of his brothers.

A king named Saul was ruler of the Israelites. David and his family were Israelites too. The Israelites were fighting with another group of people called the Philistines. David's older brothers were going off to fight. But David was too young. After helping them pack, he stayed home.

One day David's father asked him to take food to his older brothers, who were soldiers in King Saul's army.

"Visit the Israelite camp," said David's father. "And come back with news about how your brothers are doing."

"I will," David said.

King Saul's army was camped on one side of a valley. The Philistine army was gathered on the other side of the valley. David searched among Saul's soldiers until he found two of his brothers.

"What are you doing here?" asked David's oldest brother.

"This is no place for boys," his other brother said. "You should be at home with the sheep."

Just then, a giant soldier from the Philistine army stepped forward. He was nearly ten feet tall.

"I am Goliath," the giant roared. "Who is brave enough to fight me?"

None of King Saul's soldiers answered. They were all too afraid.

David was not afraid of Goliath.

"I will fight the giant," David said.

David went to King Saul and told him that he would fight Goliath.

"But you are just a boy," King Saul said. "And Goliath is a great warrior."

David told the king about how he protected his father's sheep. Finally, King Saul agreed to let David fight the giant. King Saul gave David a sword and armor to protect him. But the armor was too big.

"I cannot move in this," David said. "I will fight without armor."

David went to the stream and gathered several stones for his sling.

When Goliath saw David approaching with only a sling, the giant laughed.

"You cannot beat me," Goliath said. "You are just a boy."

"You are bigger than me," David said. "But God is on my side."

David placed a stone in his sling and sent it flying through the air. It hit Goliath right between the eyes. Goliath fell down to the ground with a loud thud.

When the Philistines saw Goliath fall, they turned and ran away. The Israelites cheered David for saving his people. Years later, David became king of Israel.

David was too young to fight. He watched the sheep and helped his older brothers pack instead. Can you find everything you see in this box somewhere in the town?

David's father told him to find food to bring to the Israelite camp. He also told him to find news about how his brothers were doing. Can you find everything you see in this box somewhere in the house?

David found rocks for his sling. He found the courage to fight Goliath with no armor. David beat Goliath with his rocks and sling! Can you find everything you see in this box somewhere in the valley?

Jonah and the Whale

Once there was a man named Jonah. When God spoke, Jonah listened. Then Jonah spread God's message to other people.

One day God told Jonah to go to the city of Nineveh. "Tell the people of Nineveh to stop being bad," said God. "They need to obey my rules."

But Jonah did not want to go to Nineveh. Instead he ran away. Jonah boarded a ship going far away from Nineveh. He fell fast asleep below the ship's deck.

While he was asleep, God sent a mighty storm to get Jonah's attention. God was angry at Jonah for disobeying him. The waves crashed and the wind blew, but still Jonah slept.

The storm got worse and worse. The sailors were afraid the ship would break apart. They all cried out to their gods to save them. But the storm raged on.

"Throw the cargo overboard," the captain yelled.

So the sailors threw the cargo into the sea. But the storm only grew stronger.

Finally, the captain went below deck to wake Jonah.

"How can you sleep in a storm like this?" asked the captain. "Pray to your God to save us!"

Then Jonah realized the storm was a message from God. Jonah knew it was his fault the ship was caught in such a terrible storm.

"Throw me overboard," said Jonah. "Then the storm will calm down."

The sailors threw Jonah into the sea. The storm suddenly calmed down. Jonah tried to swim to shore, but it was too far away. He grew very tired.

Just as Jonah sank beneath the waves, God sent a giant whale to save him. The whale swallowed Jonah whole.

Inside the belly of the whale, it was cold and smelly. Jonah was afraid. So he prayed to God.

Jonah asked God for forgiveness for not going to Nineveh. He prayed for God's help to get out of the whale.

After three days, God answered Jonah's prayer. The whale spat Jonah out onto dry land. Jonah thanked God for saving his life.

Jonah finally went to Nineveh. He told the people all about God. They listened and changed their ways.

The captain found Jonah sleeping below the ship's deck and woke him up. Jonah realized the storm was a message from God. Can you find everything you see in this box somewhere in the boat?

The sailors threw Jonah into the sea. Jonah found a whale, and the whale swallowed Jonah whole! Can you find everything you see in this box somewhere in the picture?

Jonah found other creatures in the belly of the whale. It was a cold and smelly place. But Jonah prayed and God saved him! Can you find everything you see in this box somewhere in the belly of the whale?

Daniel and the Lions

Once there was a man named Daniel who loved God. Daniel prayed to God every day. King Darius liked Daniel. He chose Daniel as one of his three advisers to help him rule the kingdom. Daniel worked hard and soon became the king's favorite.

"I think I will put Daniel in charge of everything," King Darius said one day. The other advisers were jealous of Daniel.

"Who does Daniel think he is?" one moaned. "Why should he be in charge of everything?"

"I wish he would make a big mistake," grumbled the other. "Then we could get rid of him!"

So the advisers made an evil plan.

The two advisers went to see King Darius.

"You are such a great and wise king," one cried. "You are like a god."

"You should make a new law," the other suggested. "Everyone must pray only to you. If anyone breaks the law, they will be thrown in the lions' den."

King Darius agreed to make the law. When Daniel heard about the law, he thought the other advisers might be trying to get rid of him. But Daniel still prayed to God as he always did.

The two advisers were delighted when they caught Daniel praying to God instead of to King Darius. They rushed off to tell the king.

"Daniel has broken the law!" one yelled.

"Throw him in the lions' den!" the other cried.

King Darius was sorry for making the law. He realized it was a trick to get rid of Daniel. He did not want to throw Daniel in the lions' den. But the law had to be obeyed.

"I am sorry, but you must be punished," King Darius told Daniel with tears in his eyes. "I hope your God will protect you."

Daniel was thrown into the lions' den. He kept his faith in God. Daniel prayed to God to keep him safe.

All night long, King Darius worried about Daniel. He could not eat or sleep. Early the next morning, the king rushed to the lions' den.

"Daniel, has your God saved you from the lions?" the king shouted nervously.

"Yes," Daniel replied. "God kept me safe, because he knew I did nothing wrong."

Daniel climbed out of the lions' den. He did not have a single scratch! The king was amazed that God saved Daniel.

King Darius knew the mean advisers had tricked him into punishing Daniel. So the king punished the bad men. King Darius made a new law for everyone in the kingdom to respect God. Daniel returned to helping the king rule again.

The other advisors did not like Daniel. They made an evil plan to get rid of Daniel. Can you find everything you see in this box somewhere in the throne room?

Daniel prayed to God to keep him safe in the lions' den. The next morning, King Darius found God protected Daniel from the lions. King Darius made a new law to respect God! Can you find everything you see in this box somewhere in the lions' den?

The Prodigal Son

There once was a man with two sons. They lived on a big farm. The older son worked hard and always obeyed his father. The younger son did not like to work. He wanted to travel and have fun.

One day the younger son said to his father, "Give me money so I can leave." His father agreed.

Shortly after that, the younger son packed his bags and left home. The older son stayed home to help with the farm.

The young man moved to a distant land, eager to spend his newfound wealth. He wasted money on wild parties and sinful living. Soon all his money was gone. He had no money for food.

The only job he could find was feeding pigs. The young man was so hungry that even the pigs' food looked good to eat.

"Back home, even the servants have plenty of food," he thought. "Here I am starving!"

Finally, the son understood his mistake.

"I will go home and ask Father for forgiveness," he thought. "I will ask him to hire me as a servant."

The son left for home at once. While he was still a long way off, the father saw his son approaching. He was filled with joy. The father ran to his son and hugged him.

"Forgive me, Father," the son said. "I have sinned against heaven and against you. I am no longer worthy of being called your son."

But the father welcomed his son home with open arms.

"Bring my finest clothes and dress him," the father told his servants. "We will celebrate with a party!"

Meanwhile, the older son was working in the fields. When he returned home, he heard music and laughter. He asked a servant what was happening.

"Your father is throwing a party celebrating your brother's safe return," the servant said. The older son was furious. The father came out and asked him to join the party.

"I stayed here serving you all these years. Yet you never once threw me a party," the son said. "But when my brother comes home after wasting your money, you throw him a party!"

"You are always with me and everything I have is yours," the father said. "But your brother was lost and now he is found."

Just like the father in the story, God always welcomes us home again.

The older son worked hard and obeyed his father, but the younger son wanted to travel and party. Can you find everything you see in this box somewhere in the field?

The younger son traveled and found wild parties in a distant land. Soon he wasted all his money. He had no money for food! Can you find everything you see in this box somewhere at the party?

The older son found out about the party celebrating his brother's return. He was mad at his father! But the father said he loved both of his sons. Can you find everything you see in this box somewhere in the picture?

The Birth of Jesus

Once there was a young woman named Mary who lived in the town of Nazareth. Mary was engaged to be married to a carpenter named Joseph.

One day God sent an angel to give Mary some important news. "You will have a baby boy, and you will name him Jesus," the angel said. "He will be the Son of God."

Mary was confused, but she trusted God. Joseph trusted God too. They agreed to take care of God's special son.

Around this time, the emperor in Rome made a law. The law said that everyone must go to their own hometown to register and pay taxes.

Joseph was from Bethlehem, so that is where he had to go. Mary was soon to have her baby, but she traveled to Bethlehem with Joseph anyway.

Mary and Joseph arrived in Bethlehem at night. All the inns were full. They stayed in a stable with the animals since there was no other room for them.

Mary's son was born that night. She named him Jesus as the angel told her. Mary wrapped him in a blanket and placed him in a manger. A bright star shone over the place where Jesus lay.

On that same night, some shepherds were watching over their sheep. An angel appeared. The shepherds were frightened.

"Do not be afraid," the angel said. "I bring you great news. A savior is born in Bethlehem tonight. He is Christ the Lord. You will find him lying in a manger."

Suddenly, the whole sky lit up with many angels. The angels said, "Glory to God and peace on Earth!"

After the angels left, the shepherds said to one another, "Let us go to Bethlehem. Let us find this baby."

The shepherds hurried to Bethlehem. They found Jesus lying in a manger, just as the angel told them. The shepherds bowed down and worshipped Jesus. After they left, the shepherds told everyone the good news.

Some wise men from far away saw a bright star in the sky. They followed the star all the way to the place where Jesus lay. The wise men brought Jesus gifts of gold, frankincense, and myrrh. They worshipped Jesus.

An angel warned Joseph in a dream that Bethlehem was not safe for Jesus. The angel said that Egypt was safe. So Joseph, Mary, and Jesus left for Egypt.

The angel told the shepherds the savior was born that night. The shepherds went to Bethlehem to find baby Jesus. He would bring peace on Earth! Can you find everything you see in this box somewhere in the field?

The shepherds and wise men found Jesus lying in the manger. The wise men brought gifts to Jesus and worshipped him. Can you find everything you see in this box somewhere in the manger?